Operation Bunia

The Untold Story of an
Overlooked People in Africa

D1472607

Operation Bunia

The Untold Story of an Overlooked People in Africa

Dr. James J. Seymour

Revised edition 2009

Library of Congress Control Number:

ISBN: 978-1-4276-3355-2

Publishing Consultants:

Evangel Publishing House
Pvt Bag 28963-00200
Nairobi, Kenya.
info@evangelpublishing.org
www.evangelpublishing.org

Cover Design Consultant: Hal Bredbenner

Additional copies of this book are available by mail.
Suggested donation of $12.00 for each copy including shipping and handling.
      Contact: Accumulated Resources
             333 E. Six Forks Road Suite 105
             Raleigh, North Carolina 27609 USA
             Email: jims@arks.org

Contents

Acknowledgements

I want to thank those who worked so hard to assist me in the development of this book. I would like to thank the administration of Saint Augustine's College who have allowed me some latitude in my schedule to be in Africa twice each year, and encouraged me to pursue my work on the continent of Africa. I am proud to serve at an institution that seeks to make the entire world a better place for all.

I would like to thank Robert Knowles, President of Arks Funding LLC for seeing the value of this project and also the various projects we are doing in Africa. I would like to thank the Farrell Foundation for their investment in the many works in Africa. I would like to thank my wife Dawn for her proof reading skills and insight. I also want to thank my friend of over thirty years, Steve Briggs, for his many hours of editing as well as my two administrative assistants Ginny Huff at ARKS, and Tenisha Robinson at Saint Augustine's College.

I want to express my appreciation to Natalie Bullock-Brown for her artistic contribution to this book, Hal Bredbenner for technical assistance, and my co-worker in the DR Congo, Jean Paul Drata, for gathering the stories of his people in Bunia.

Dedication

I would like to dedicate this book to the four million men, women, and children of the Democratic Republic of Congo who lost their lives during the years of war and conflict in their nation. This book is but a meager attempt to honor your memory and pray that others will never have to pay your price for peace.

About the Author

Dr. James J. Seymour has earned a Doctor of Ministry Degree and a Master of Divinity Degree from Faith Evangelical Seminary. He also has a Masters Degree in Community/Agency Counseling from Fairfield University, a Bachelors Degree in History from Southeastern University, a Ministerial Diploma from Zion Bible College, and a Certificate in Non-Profit Management from Duke University.

Introduction

TOUCHING PAIN, BIRTHING VISION, DISPENSING HOPE

Over the last thirty years I have had an abiding love for the continent of Africa and her people. My love and respect for the inhabitants of this vast continent includes those descendants who came to the shores of America during the 17th, 18th, and 19th centuries during the Atlantic slave trade. Out of Africa we behold a people who have had to survive the perils of slavery, the indignities of colonialism, the seeming hopelessness of Jim Crow segregation in the American South, and a courageous battle for Civil Rights that has given hope to freedom loving people across the world. Both the African and African American people have my deepest admiration and respect. Serving them is my life's ambition.

My family and I moved to the nation of Zimbabwe in Southern Africa in February of 1980, two months before the first election of an African leader for the nation previously known by its colonial name, Rhodesia. Robert Gabriel Mugabe was elected as Prime Minister and after the political system changed several years later, he became the President. We were as a family privileged to grow with the people of this newly born nation as they worked through the transition of self governance.

Colonialism did little to prepare for its legitimate successors to lead and rule and become a part of the international community. One of the great tragedies of post-colonial Africa is the corruption of many of her leaders and their failure to put the needs of the people over their own personal ambitions.

I have been involved in several African nations in various roles serving as a missionary, educator, counselor, and humanitarian roles. Zimbabwe has always been my "first love" among the many nations I have visited to teach or serve in. The people of Zimbabwe treated my family with great love and respect and embraced us as their own. My children grew up there and my youngest daughter was born there and now, as an adult, lives and serves on the continent of her birth in the nation of Madagascar.

We have life-long friendships with many people of Zimbabwe. However, over the last several years my heart has been deeply touched as I have been involved with the courageous people of another great African nation, the Democratic Republic of Congo.

In recent years Africa has experienced some horrific tragedies that have stunned the world due to their violence and magnitude. In Rwanda between mid-April and mid- July of 1994, a timeline of around 100 days, between 800,000 and 1,000,000 people died in the tribal violence between the Hutu and Tutsi. The world was astounded by the pictures, reports, and the subsequent movie, Hotel Rwanda, that brought this nightmare to the big screen.

In Southern Sudan two Civil Wars raged in the twentieth century. The first was from 1955-1972 and the second from 1983-2005. The conflict was largely between the Arab Muslim of the North and the African Christians of the South. This is considered the longest running Civil War of the 20th century, with some two million people losing their lives and around four million being displaced from their homes. A fragile Peace Agreement was signed in 2005 giving much autonomy to the people of Southern Sudan to set up their own government, to enjoy profit sharing from the oil wells of the south, and with the ability to hold a referendum in seven years on whether or not to reunite with the Arab north as one nation. Already there are many cracks in this tentative treaty and only time will tell if it will hold or if violence will reemerge.

The situation in Darfur in Western Sudan has been highly publicized since its inception in February of 2003. Unlike the conflict in the South which had a deep religious component, this conflict is more ethnic and tribal. Arab Muslims from the North have attacked and killed African Muslims in the Darfur region. One side of the armed conflict is composed mainly of the Sudanese military and the Janjaweed, a militia group recruited mostly from the Arab Baggara tribes of the northern Rizeigat, who are camel-herding nomads.

The other side comprises a variety of rebel groups, notably the Sudan Liberation Movement and the Justice and Equality Movement, recruited primarily from the land-tilling non-Arab Fur, Zaghawa, and Massaleit ethnic groups.

The Sudanese government, while publicly denying that it supports the Janjaweed, has provided money and assistance to the militia and has participated in joint attacks targeting the tribes from which the rebels draw support.

The involvement of some of Hollywood's most elite entertainers including George Clooney, Brad Pitt, and Angelina Jolie has shown a bright light on this terrible tragedy which the United States government has declared to be "a genocide." The look of hopelessness and fear on the faces of the women and children has shaken the world and elicited outrage by many with the inaction of the United Nations to stop this well documented evil.

Somehow overlooked in the shadow of these catastrophic humanitarian crisis' has been another, and some might say, even more horrendous situation in the Democratic Republic of Congo, the third largest nation in Africa located in the central region of the continent. The International Rescue Committee reports that between August 1998 and April 2004, when the bulk of the fighting occurred, nearly four million people died in the DRC. Most of these deaths were due to starvation or disease that resulted from the war, not from actual fighting. Millions more have become internally displaced or have sought asylum in neighboring countries.

I first visited the town of Bunia, located in the Ituri Distric in northeastern Congo in December of 2006. I was there to speak at a conference organized by the Africa Inland Church.

Some 1,000 plus people gathered for several days of teaching as Dr. JL Williams of New Directions International, Rev. Ednar Jante of Haiti, and myself were the primary speakers. What I saw over those days made a deep impression on my mind and heart. I met countless widows who had lost their husbands during the years of war and were trying desperately to survive with their children.

I witnessed children who literally lived on the streets in groups, sleeping in the shadow of buildings and never sure where they would next find food. When I climbed into the small Cessna plane to leave Bunia I resolved in my heart that, "doing nothing is not an option." Thus was born what has come to be known as, Operation Bunia.

Dr. James J. Seymour
Professor, Saint Augustine's College
Executive Director, ARKS

PART 1

A BRIEF HISTORY OF THE DEMOCRATIC REPUBLIC OF CONGO

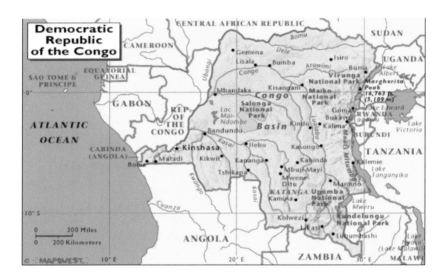

Chapter 1

COLONIALISM IN AFRICA

In an almost unprecedented act of Euro-centric arrogance a conference was called in Berlin, Germany in 1884 to discuss the dissecting of the Continent of Africa by various European nations. Typically nations had only come together in such gatherings in the aftermath of war to negotiate a peace agreement.

This gathering was a pro- active act to prevent war and conflict between European powers as they negotiated how to divide the lucrative land of Africa for their own colonial gains. The Berlin Conference has been called Africa's undoing in more ways than one. The colonial powers superimposed their domains on the African continent. By the time independence returned to Africa in 1950, the realm had acquired a legacy of political fragmentation that could neither be eliminated nor made to operate satisfactorily.

In 1884 at the request of Portugal, German Chancellor Otto von Bismark called together the major Western powers of the world to negotiate questions and end confusion over the control of Africa. The Berlin Congress produced the Berlin Act of 1885 which established the "conventional basin of the Congo," and opened it to European free trade, made it neutral in times of war, and promoted efforts to end the slave trade. This was an unprecedented piece of international diplomacy, since it included so many different countries.

The most important consequence of the Berlin Act was the reduction of tension that resulted from the French explorations in the Congo basin (Savorgnan de Brazza, 1876-1877), the establishment of Belgian posts in the Congo (1879-1884), the French invasion of Tunisia (1881), and the British takeover of Egypt (1882). In essence, the representatives agreed that rivalries over African soil were not serious enough to justify a war between European nations.

The Provisions of the Berlin Act:

- The principle of the freedom of navigation was established on the Niger and Congo Rivers, without prejudice to existing establishments. In practice, this meant that everyone could sail on the two rivers, but they had to pay the owners of existing posts for the right to dock and trade there.

- The limits of the Portuguese claims in Angola and Mozambique were defined, and French claims along the Congo River were recognized.

- Leopold's "International Association of the Congo" was recognized as the de facto government of the Congo basin, and the territory was renamed "The Congo Free State."

In the long run, the Berlin Congress stimulated the, "Scramble for Africa" by establishing rules for the recognition of European claims. In brief, after signing the Berlin Act, a European nation could no longer simply raise its flag along the African coast and claim everything that lay behind it in the hinterland.

Instead, a European colonial power had to physically occupy whatever it claimed with troops, missionaries, merchants, or better yet, railroads, forts, and buildings. At the time of the conference, 80% of Africa remained under traditional and local control. What ultimately resulted was the establishment of new boundaries that now divided Africa into fifty irregular countries. This new map of the continent was thrust forcefully upon the one thousand indigenous cultures and regions of Africa.

The new countries forced together tribes who were ancient rivals under the banner of a new nation. It is not surprising that for many in Africa tribal loyalties supercede national loyalty as they never chose to be a part of one nation in the first place. By 1902, 90% of all the land that makes up Africa was under European control. In less than twenty years, Africa was under foreign domination.

Fourteen countries were represented by a vast array of ambassadors when the conference opened in Berlin on November 15, 1884. The countries represented at the time included Austria, Hungary, Belgium, Denmark, France, Germany, Great Britain, Italy, the Netherlands, Portugal, Russia, Spain, Sweden, Norway, Turkey, and the United States of America. Of these fourteen nations, France, Germany, Great Britain, and Portugal were the major players in the conference, controlling most of colonial Africa at the time.

The initial task of the conference was to agree that the Congo River and Niger River mouths and basins would be considered neutral and open to trade.

Despite its neutrality, part of the Congo Basin became a personal kingdom for Belgium's King Leopold II and during his rule, over half of the region's population died under the tyranny of being forced to work without wages on rubber plantations to further the wealth of the King.

At the time of the conference, only the coastal areas of Africa were colonized by the European powers. At the Berlin Conference the European colonial powers scrambled to gain control over the interior of the continent. The conference lasted until February 26, 1885.

During this three month period the colonial powers negotiated over boundaries in the interior of the continent, while totally disregarding the cultural and linguistic boundaries already established by the indigenous African population.

By 1914, the conference participants had fully divided Africa among themselves into fifty countries. The success of the colonial powers led to the destruction of African cultures and lifestyles in ways that would be lost perhaps forever.

Major Colonial Holdings Included:

- Great Britain desired a Cape-to-Cairo collection of colonies and almost succeeded though their control of Egypt, Sudan (Anglo-Egyptian Sudan), Uganda, Kenya (British East Africa), South Africa, Zambia, Zimbabwe (Rhodesia), and Botswana. The British also controlled Nigeria and Ghana (Gold Coast).

- France took much of western Africa, from Mauritania to Chad (French West Africa) and Gabon and the Republic of Congo (French Equatorial Africa).

- Belgium and King Leopold II controlled the Democratic Republic of Congo (Belgian Congo).

- Portugal took Mozambique in the east and Angola in the west.

- Italy's holdings were Somalia (Italian Somaliland) and a portion of Ethiopia.

- Germany took Namibia (German Southwest Africa) and Tanzania (German East Africa).

- Spain claimed the smallest territory - Equatorial Guinea (Rio Muni).

The colonial era was now unleashed in all its fury and the lust for land and power seemed insatiable. With little or no regard for the indigenous people of Africa, European businessmen, settlers, farmers, missionaries, and military forces simply took over a continent that was not their own by birth, but now belonged to them through force. It would take nearly 100 years for Africans to regain even a semblance of political and economic control over the land of their forefathers.

It is very offensive to the people of Africa in the 21st Century to find so little compassion or understanding from the nations of the West as they face post-colonial struggles. Few in Europe or America have taken the time to study the impact of colonialism on the actual people of

Africa. For moral reasons alone there must be a sense of responsibility from the West to seek to help the people of Africa.

Chapter 2

ONE LAND WITH MANY NAMES

The Belgian Congo

On November 15, 1908, King Léopold II of Belgium formally relinquished personal control of the Congo Free State, and the renamed Belgian Congo came under the administration of the Belgian parliament, a system which lasted until independence was granted in 1960. The Belgian administration might be most charitably characterized as paternalistic colonialism. The educational system was dominated by the Roman Catholic Church and Protestant churches and the curricula reflected Christian and Western values. For example, in 1948 fully 99.6% of educational facilities were controlled by Christian missions.

The Congo Crisis (1960–1965)

Patrice Lumumba

Political administration fell under the total and direct control of the mother country. There were no democratic institutions. Native curfews and other restrictions were not unusual. Following World War II some democratic reforms began to be introduced, but these were complicated by ethnic rivalries among the native population.

Following a series of riots and unrest, the Belgians realized they could not maintain control of such a vast country. The Belgians announced on January 27, 1960 that they would relinquish control in six months. The Congo was granted its independence on June 30, 1960, adopting the name "Republic of the Congo" (République du Congo). As the French colony of Middle Congo (Moyen Congo) also chose the name Republic of Congo upon receiving its independence, the two countries were more commonly known as Congo-Léopoldville and Congo-Brazzaville, after their capital cities. In 1966, Joseph Désiré Mobutu changed the country's official name to Zaire.

At the time of independence, the country was in a very unstable state as regional tribal leaders held far more power than the central government, and with the departure of the Belgian administrators there were almost no skilled bureaucrats left in the country.

The first Congolese university graduate was only in 1956, and virtually no one in the new nation had any idea of how to manage a country of such size. Parliamentary elections in 1960 produced the nationalist Patrice Lumumba as Prime Minister and pro-Western Joseph Kasavubu as President of the renamed, Democratic Republic of the Congo.

From the very beginning of its existence democracy began to unravel. A military coup broke out in the capital and rampant looting began. On July 11th the richest province of the country, Katanga, seceded under Moise Tshombe. To protect Europeans in the country and try to restore order 20,000 UN peacekeepers were sent to the country. Western paramilitaries and mercenaries often hired by mining companies to protect their interests also began to pour into the country. In this same period Congo's second richest province, Kasai, also announced its independence.

Prime Minister Lumumba turned to the USSR for assistance. Nikita Khrushchev agreed to help, offering advanced weaponry and technical advisors. The United States viewed the Soviet presence as an attempt to take advantage of the situation and gain a proxy state in sub-Saharan Africa. UN forces were ordered to block any shipments of arms into the country. The United States also looked for a way to replace Lumumba as leader. President Kasavubu had clashed with Prime Minister Lumumba and advocated an alliance with the West rather than the Soviets. The U.S. sent weapons and CIA personnel to aid forces allied with Kasavubu and combat the Soviet presence.

In December 1960, with U.S. and CIA support, Kasavubu and his loyal Colonel Joseph Mobutu overthrew the government. Lumumba was assassinated by Mobutu. According to some allegations both the United States and the Belgian government were in support of such an action. After some reverses, UN and Congolese government forces succeeded in recapturing the breakaway provinces of Katanga and South Kasai. In Stanleyville, those loyal to the deposed Lumumba set up a rival government under Antoine Gizenga. This rebellion was ended with the help of Belgian, British, and US troops.

Zaire (1965–1996)

Mobutu Sese Seko

Unrest and rebellion plagued the government until 1965, when Lieutenant General Mobutu, by then commander in chief of the national army, seized control of the country and declared that he would be the president for five years.

Mobutu quickly consolidated his power and was elected unopposed as president in 1970. Embarking on a campaign of cultural awareness, Mobutu renamed the country the Republic of Zaire and required citizens to adopt African names. Relative peace and stability prevailed until 1977 and 1978 when Katangan rebels, based in Angola, launched a series of invasions into the Shaba (Katanga) region. The rebels were driven out with the aid of Belgian paratroopers.

During the 1980s, Zaire remained a one-party state. Although Mobutu successfully maintained control during this period, opposition parties, most notably the Union pour la Démocratie et le Progrès Social (UDPS), were active. Mobutu's attempts to quell these groups drew significant international criticism.

As the Cold War came to a close, internal and external pressures on Mobutu increased. In late 1989 and early 1990, Mobutu was weakened by a series of domestic protests, heightened international criticism of his regime's human rights practices, a faltering economy, government corruption, and most notably his massive embezzlement of government funds for personal use.

In April 1990, Mobutu declared the Third Republic, agreeing to a limited multi-party system with elections and a constitution. As details of a reform package were delayed, soldiers in September 1991 began looting Kinshasa to protest their unpaid wages. Two thousand French and Belgian troops, some of whom were flown in on U.S. Air Force planes, arrived to evacuate the 20,000 endangered foreign nationals in Kinshasa.

In 1992, after previous similar attempts, the long-promised Sovereign National Conference was staged, encompassing over 2,000 representatives from various political parties. The conference gave itself a legislative mandate and elected Archbishop Laurent Monsengwo as its chairman, along with Étienne Tshisekedi wa Mulumba, leader of the UDPS, as Prime Minister. By the end of the year Mobutu had created a rival government with its own Prime Minister.

The ensuing stalemate produced a compromise merger of the two governments into the High Council of Republic-Parliament of Transition in 1994, with Mobutu as Head of State and Kengo Wa Dondo as Prime Minister. Although presidential and legislative elections were scheduled repeatedly over the next two years, they never took place.

War and Transition (1996–2006)

By 1996, tension and genocide from the neighboring Rwanda war had spilled over to Zaire. The Rwandan Hutu militia forces known as Interahamwe fled Rwanda following the ascension of a Tutsi-led government. The Hutu militia had been using Hutu tribal refugees' camps in eastern Zaire as a basis for incursion against Rwanda. Hutu militia forces soon allied with the Zairian armed forces (FAZ) to launch a campaign against Congolese ethnic Tutsis in eastern Zaire. In turn, the Tutsis formed a militia to defend themselves against attacks. When the Zairian government began to escalate its massacres in November 1996, the Tutsi militias erupted in rebellion against Mobutu.

The Tutsi militia was soon joined by various opposition groups and supported by several countries, including Rwanda and Uganda. This coalition, led by Laurent-Desire Kabila, became known as the Alliance des Forces Démocratiques pour la Libération du Congo-Zaïre (AFDL). The AFDL, now seeking the broader goal of ousting Mobutu, made significant military gains in early 1997.

Following failed peace talks between Mobutu and Kabila in May 1997, Mobutu left the country, and Kabila marched unopposed to Kinshasa on May 20. Kabila named himself president, consolidated power around himself and the AFDL, and returned the name of the country to the Democratic Republic of Congo.

Kabila struggled with the challenges of managing the problems of his country. He lost his allies and the Mouvement pour la Libération du Congo. The MLC was led by the warlord Jean-Pierre Bemba, who would be a source of conflict for years to come. Rwandan and Ugandan troops attacked in August 1998, soon after Angola, Zimbabwe, and Namibia sent some forces into the DRC to support the government.

While the six African governments involved in the war signed a ceasefire accord in Lusaka in July 1999, the Congolese rebels did not sign. The ceasefire broke down within months of the signing. Kabila was assassinated in January 2001 by one of his own bodyguards. He was succeeded by his son Joseph, who upon taking office, called for multilateral peace talks to end the war.

Joseph Kabila partly succeeded in February 2001 when a further peace deal was brokered between Kabila, Rwanda, and Uganda, leading to the apparent withdrawal of foreign troops. UN peacekeepers MONUC arrived in April 2001.

Talks between Kabila and the rebel leaders lasted a full six weeks, beginning in April 2002. In June they signed a peace accord in which Kabila would share power with former rebels.

By June 2003 all foreign armies except those of Rwanda had pulled out of Congo. As the civil war continued between the government and the different rebel groups, an ethnic conflict between the Hema and Lendu tribes erupted in 1999 in the Ituri district of the Oriental Province of Eastern Congo. This violence continued until 2004, resulting in the loss of over 80,000 lives and a systematic destruction of public infrastructures such as schools, hospitals, and churches.

The Hema tribe is said to have been backed by the Rwandan troops while the Lendu were backed by the Ugandan troops. These foreign troops have been accused of looting the mineral resources, particularly the gold, from the Mongwalu gold mines, coltan, cattle and timber from the wealthy Ituri District. Ethnic clashes in the northeast were still taking place in 2004, especially violence between the Hema and Lendu tribes in the Kivu region of Eastern Congo.

President Joseph Kabila Taking His Oath of Office

A constitution was approved by voters and on July 30, 2006 the Democratic Republic of Congo held its first multi-party elections since independence in 1960. Joseph Kabila took 45% of the votes and his opponent Jean-Pierre Bemba took 20%. This result was the catalyst for a fight between the two factions, from August 20-22, 2006 in the streets of the capital, Kinshasa. Sixteen people died before policemen and UN mission forces known as MONUC took control of the city.

A second election run off was organized to satisfy the constitution, which stipulates that the winner should gather at least 51% of the vote. In the second national election, on October 29, 2006, Kabila won with 70% of the votes. Bemba has made multiple public statements saying the election had "irregularities," despite the fact that every neutral observer had praised the elections.

On December 6, 2006, the Transitional Government came to an end. Joseph Kabila was sworn in as the first democratically elected President in over forty years. A new era of fragile hope and tentative aspirations was born.

Despite the military presence of the largest UN force in the world, the Congo is far from experiencing peace. The multiple rebel movements contribute to the unrest and terror among the poor, especially in the Kivu Providence and the Ituri District. The self-proclaimed General Nkunda Batware has been terrorizing the weak and frail citizens in the Masisi region, leading to the creation of a community based defense movement commonly called Mai Mai.

Different warlords have been using systematic rape, looting, and abduction in order to create terror in the lives of the helpless citizens. Rape cases go on at a rate of some one thousand per month in these two regions alone. Children as young as eight years old, have been forced to join the rebel forces and their future sacrificed. Clearly there is still much work to be done to achieve genuine peace and stability for all citizens.

Chapter 3

CORRUPTION AND EXPLOITATION OF NATURAL RESOURCES

According to Nicky Oppenheimer, De Beers Chairman, natural resources are morally neutral. As such they can be a source of great good or dreadful ill. The key element is not the resource itself, but how it is exploited, and Africa provides telling examples of both. An orderly mining regime, operating within a transparent and predictable legislative and fiscal framework, can be a major source of prosperity for governments and people.

Without it, mineral wealth, especially, but not exclusively in its more accessible forms, will be a magnet for the greedy and corrupt to line their own pockets at the expense of the people. Once the rot has set in, it is virtually unstoppable, until the entire fabric of economic and social development has been completely eroded.' Thus the dilemma of the mineral wealth of the Democratic Republic of Congo has brought more heartache then prosperity to the majority of the people of the nation.

The history of the Congo since the late 19th century has provided ample examples of how the unprincipled exploitation of natural resources can give rise to human rights abuses. It has also demonstrated how corruption or the mismanagement of natural resources can undermine a country's development and hence the enjoyment by its citizens of their social and economic rights.

Self-serving leadership geared toward the personal enrichment of the ruling elite at the expense of the general population has had an enormously negative impact on the country and its citizens through the years. Congolese often say, "We'd be so much better off if we weren't so rich." The great wealth of this unhappy territory at the center of Africa has long attracted foreigners. Centuries ago Atlantic slave traders anchored in the mouth of the Congo River and filled their ships with captives from the interior. Today's predators are African armies and European and American corporations hungering for mineral wealth.

The territory has a long history of plunder. After the slave trade ended, ivory and rubber made Congo the bloodiest European colony in Africa. It was the real-life setting for Joseph Conrad's book, "Heart of Darkness." As noted in previously, for twenty three years it was the private property of King Leopold II of Belgium, who made a huge fortune by turning most adult male Congolese into slaves to gather wild rubber. His private army worked hundreds of thousands of men to death, and brutally suppressed twenty years of uprisings.

Just as today, disease took the greatest toll, ravaging a traumatized, half-starving people, many of whom hid unsheltered in the rain forest. Demographers estimate that the population was cut by half - a loss of some 10 million people - during Leopold's rule and its immediate aftermath.

In 1908, the Belgian government took over the colony, and gradually the carnage slowed and stopped. However, as in much of colonial Africa, forced labor remained, and mining profits flowed overseas. For most of the years since Congo's abrupt independence in 1960, the dictator Mobutu Sese Seko ruled the country with U.S. support, and with more than one billion dollars in U.S. aid. With his remote marble palace, his love of pink champagne, chartered Concord's, and his luxury homes dotted around Europe, Mobutu and his entourage plundered the country of an estimated four billion dollars before being overthrown in 1997.

Afterwards the Congo slid quickly into war. Seeing a huge, resource-rich country with no functioning government, neighboring countries joined in dividing the spoils. At various points, the armies of seven nations - most importantly Rwanda, Uganda, and Zimbabwe - have had troops on Congo's soil. The Rwandan army stole natural resources worth $250 million in 1999 and 2000 alone, according to a UN report. Even after most foreign troops went home, their commanders retained lucrative mineral concessions and an ever-changing web of alliances.

These companies have been eagerly buying Congo's diamonds, gold, timber, copper, cobalt and columbo-tantalite, which is known as "coltan". Eastern Congo, the scene of the terrible fighting during the war years, has more than half the world's supply of coltan, which is used in computer chips and cell phones, and has occasionally sold for as much, per ounce as gold.

Mining Firms Aid Congo Plunder - UN Expert

In a Reuters report on October 25, 2002 the chief author of a UN study on the plundering of Congo's riches said that big mining firms, despite denials, played a crucial role in the looting of the African nation's gems and minerals. "The role of these companies is really important," according to Egyptian Mahmoud Kassem, chairman of a panel of UN experts whose report on the pillaging of the Democratic Republic of Congo's natural resources .

Kassem declared, "Corporations have a direct and indirect role. Without them, this kind of commerce would not be possible," he told a news conference, emphasizing everything in the report had been cor- roborated before publication. The panel's report said the systematic pillaging continued unabated by the military in Rwanda, Uganda, and Zimbabwe, aided by Congolese government officials and criminal networks.

The panel called on the United Nations to impose financial restric- tions on 29 companies and 54 individuals involved in the pillaging. It also named 85 multinational mining firms as well as banks in South

Africa, Europe, Canada and the United States, accusing them of ignoring OECD guidelines on ethics and dealings with human rights abusers.

Mining giants around the world quickly rejected allegations of "mineral rape" in the DR Congo, whose inhabitants are desperately poor though it is home to some of the world's richest mineral resources. Global mining giant Anglo American PLC told Reuters it has had no operations in the Congo since the 1960s.

Diamond king De Beers added there was nothing in the report to substantiate the allegations, and Canadian miner First Quantum Minerals asked for a full retraction. As accusations and denials are hurled back and forth, the people of the DR Congo struggle to survive just one day at a time.

PART 11

PROFILES OF COURAGE

The following stories are told by people I have come to know and love over the last several years. In their own words they tell of their loss, their suffering, and their hope as they bravely face an uncertain future after a stunningly painful past. It is important to read their words carefully, but even more essential to listen intently to their hearts

Chapter 4

THE PEOPLE OF BUNIA: COURAGE IN THE MIDST OF CRISIS

The fundamental element that distinguishes conflicts in traditional African societies from those in the Western world is the cultural setting. The ways African individuals and groups handle disputes between themselves is, in many significant ways, unlike those in the west. In addition, the methods that are effective for resolving conflicts also differ. Westerners make many mistakes in judgment when dealing with conflict encounters unless they have taken time to understand these differences.

Pastor Jean Marc Ubukandi ... The Trail of Tears

Pastor Jean Marc and wife with daughters Grace and Merry

Bullet holes mark the outside wall of the house

Through a Daughters Eyes

I am Nyeligudi Merry-Valentine, 26 years of age, from Bunia, a small town in northeastern Democratic Republic of Congo. I am the second born in a family of four. My parents are servants of God. My father is the assistant pastor of the French Parish known as, "La Paroisse Francophone, CECA-20 Bunia." By the grace of God I have been able to complete my Bachelors' Degree in Counseling Psychology from Pan Africa Christian University in Nairobi on 21 July 2007.

Presently, I am doing my Masters in International Relations at United States International University Africa (USIU) in Nairobi Kenya. This is the story of my family's survival during a time of war.

The Lord's Mercy

Beginning in the year 2001 a seemingly endless political and tribal instability troubled my home area causing much destruction of property and many people lost their lives. This madness took the life of my own elder brother and destroyed everything in our home. The Lord has been so gracious and merciful to the rest of my family despite the many challenges. My family was among many others who almost lost hope for the future due to the effects of the war that had reached the common man to the point where people were feeling completely helpless.

My Family's Eleven Day Walk for Survival

In June 2003, my 28 years old brother was killed at the door of our home in the presence of the rest of the family in Bunia. The situation was unbearable and consequently, my parents and little sisters had to leave my brother's body alone in the house and escape for their lives. The body was buried by some young men of our community. None of my family members witnessed or knew were it was buried. For an African family this is a tragedy beyond words.

My family walked through the forest for eleven days together with other displaced persons. They walked from Bunia to Beni in the far eastern part of the country, a total of 300 kilometers (186 miles).

The experience in the forest was not a good one. When the night came as they walked though the forest they would rest by sleeping on leaves and often were rained on. Because of the lack of food my father once traded his shirt for something to eat for the children.

Due to the horrible conditions, my little son Joseph, one and half years old at that time, became very ill in the forest. Everybody lost hope that he could survive. Fortunately God intervened in a miraculous way. The African Inland Church missionaries sent an airplane to come and pick up the Bishop who was also among the crowd in the forest. When he saw the condition of my little boy, he decided to give his own seat in the plane for my mother and little Joseph to be taken to hospital in Beni. That is how his life was saved. I am so very thankful to God for sparing the life of my parents, my sisters, and my son.

One month later, some AIC missionary friends organized to take my family with many others to the AIC center in Nairobi, Kenya to rest and heal from their trauma. After six months my father, overwhelmed with concern for the rest of the flock back in Bunia, had to go back. Therefore, they left Nairobi and went back home so start life from point zero. Since that time little by little and day by day they have begun to rebuild their lives and prepare for an uncertain future. They prayed for peace, and that the days of war will recede into a painful but distant memory.

James Byensi...An Inheritance of Orphans

The Democratic Republic of Congo has one of the saddest stories in recent world history, with more deaths than any nation since World War II. People are still talking about the 1994 genocide in Rwanda when 800,000 people died in 90 days. Much is being said about the Darfur conflict where 200,000 people have lost their lives in the last several years. There has been much attention accorded to the post election skirmishes in Kenya in January 2008 with the death of some 2,000 citizens.

While truly all of these situations are very painful and tragic, none of the above mentioned conflicts reach in any way to the level of the atrocities DR Congo has experienced. The twelve year conflict in Congo has so far claimed over 5.4 millions lives. Innocent people have fallen to bullets, machetes, rape, or by diseases such as malaria and malnutrition as an aftermath of war.

The Ituri district, my homeland, remains the bloodiest corner of this vast nation. Ituri alone has so far lost over 100,000 of its precious sons and daughters to the tribal clashes between the Hema and Lendu tribes and also in politically motivated conflicts. Worse still, more people continue to die each day because of the unending political unrest in the land. With the loss of lives follows a systematic looting and destruction of both private and public infrastructures such as houses, businesses, cattle, schools, hospitals, churches, roads, bridges, radio stations just to mention a few.

The essential question is, "Does the Democratic Republic of Congo still exists on the international map?" If the answer is yes than why have we faced this appalling silence from the rest of the world? Where has the international media gone? Is the international community guilty of its passive or negative involvement in the conflict? History and ultimately God will one day judge this reality.

I am James Byensi, and I have lost 17 close relatives in this madness. The latest victim was my beloved mother Evanissi who could not bear the trauma any longer. I lost my two elder brothers, one brother-in-law, several cousins and nephews in the conflict.

We lost everything we have ever worked for including family houses, business and farm, hundreds of cattle, and much more. One day's strike was enough to ruin everything that had been earned for generations. Today I have inherited personal misery plus eleven orphans and two widows to take care of. The question each one asks and that no one can answer is, "why did they kill our father?"

I was faced with the same question in a rescue operation I conducted in 2001 to save the lives of two little Lendu girls, one with an arrow extending through her neck, and her sister with two deep cuts in her head. These little girls, Sarah, six years old and Machozi nine years old, witnessed their parents and seven siblings cut into pieces by their neighbors in Nyankunde. They miraculously escaped and ran four kilometers despite the profuse bleeding they suffered. Thank God that they are alive today, and Sarah was adopted by a Christian family which has since found refuge in England.

Rape and abductions were other effective weapons used to terrorize the already frail and traumatized people. In 2003 my elder sister Beatrice was abducted with around 20 other people. She helplessly witnessed these dear people being killed one by one. When her turn came, a fight broke out among the assailants with some protecting her and others wanting her dead. Eventually fire exchange followed and three militiamen were killed and amazingly her life was spared. She was forced to become the commander's wife. She miraculously escaped after sixteen months though having born the commanders child.

No one believed their eyes the day she came back home after the mourning and funeral service had already taken place. My widowed elder sister Sophie also escaped death narrowly in 2005 when the truck she traveled in was ambushed by the militiamen. Seven of the twelve passengers were shot dead. She was shot in the right leg and left in the bush to bleed to death. However by God's grace she survived, though she will be lame for the rest of her life. Thousands of such disturbing stories are yet to be told.

I am well aware of the adversity my country is facing with its political instability, 10% of HIV/AIDS prevalence, over 3,000 rape cases monthly, 45,000 people dying per month, most of whom are women and children. Yet I also know that God has not forsaken the Democratic Republic of Congo and its people. It is true that remembering my afflictions my soul may be downcast. I quickly recall the Lord's compassion and mercies never fail and are new every morning. Therefore I hope in Him no matter how dry the situation may look. I remain indebted to

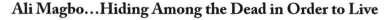

all those who in one way or the other are on the cutting edge of giving hope to the people of Congo. May God bless them.

Ali Magbo…Hiding Among the Dead in Order to Live

I am Jephthah Ali Magbo, a Congolese son of Magbo Mugenyi, a businessman and farmer in Djugu District of Ituri province, in DRC. I am 30 years old and born in a polygamous family of more than 70 children. Currently, I am a student, studying Political Science in CUEB Bunia. On July 26, 2001, I gave my life to Jesus Christ. I serve the Lord in the intercession ministry in Paroisse Ville.

I would like to share an unforgettable chapter of my life story with you. It began on March 6, 2003 and continued through May 11, 2003. Each day, I would rise early for morning prayers at church from 6:00 AM to 7:00 AM. On Thursday, March 6, 2003, we were praising the Lord through songs when we heard gun shots from the airport area. The violence continued throughout the day in all parts of the city of Bunia, yet we continued our ministry at the church.

During this time, the militias of UPC, Patriotic Union of Congolese, in coalition with the Ugandan troops, were defeated and left the city in the hands of the Lendu tribe militias. In April 2003 CPI (Ituri Pacification Commission) was created from all the communities (tribes) living in Ituri province. The commission met for 15 days, looking for ways to live in peace with one another. I represented the church, as a member of the commission. A tentative peace developed during the period that the commission met. One of the resolutions of CPI was that the Ugandan soldiers in Bunia, who were also in charge of security of the city, should leave Bunia at once.

MONUC (United Nations Mission in the Congo D.R) and other international organizations put pressure on Uganda. Finally after long discussions and negotiations Uganda accepted the plan to retrieve its military from Bunia.

The first Ugandan troop convoy left Bunia on Tuesday, May 6, 2003 around 3:00 P.M. They were followed by thousands of men, women, and children fleeing the violence that was to come. Tuesday night was unforgettable because no one was able to sleep due to the constant gun fire throughout Bunia. Even though the following morning was calm, I decided to stay in my home.

Later that day, I received the tragic news a brother in Christ was shot during the night. He had ministered with me in Youth Service at church. I believed I had no choice but to visit his family.

As I reached their home immediately there was more gun fire that started as a result of warfare between two militias. We witnessed a great number of people fleeing for their lives towards the city center, to the UN mission MONUC Headquarters. I hurried home for my safety, but the gun fire became severe. I decided to hide in the church Intercession Center near ISTB (Theological Seminary in Bunia) which is today called USB (Shalom University of Bunia). I met other brothers and sisters in Christ, at the center, praying for the city and the nation as the gun fire continued until 6:00 P.M. I spent the night at the church due to the violence.

The next morning, I rushed home, despite the danger of the

widespread violence. My concern was for the lives of my mother and others family and friends. I managed to reach home but unfortunately I found no one except our neighbors, who were removing valuables from our house to save them from pillage. They pleaded with me to leave the place as quickly as possible because it was dangerous for me to be there.

The next few days I experienced severe anxiety for my mother and family. By Saturday I began to look for them, even though I could not move around safely because of the danger. I am of the Hema tribe and Bunia was in the hands of Lendu tribe militias. Finally I found out that my "mum" and other people were safe in the airport, which was under MONUC troop control.

Now comes the most unforgettable Sunday of my life, May 11, 2003. I woke up early in the morning and prepared for church. On my way to church, I met two militia men who commanded me to stop. One of them asked, "What is your name?" I replied, "Ali Jephthah." Before I could finish, the other militias asked, "So what is your family name?" Before I said a word, he added "You are a Hema, aren't you?" Upon his question, I could not speak any more.

They commanded that I take off my trouser and shoes. "Where were you going?" they asked. I coldly replied, "I am a Christian and I am on my way to church." They didn't believe me and judged that I was a Hema militia soldier. They took me to my pastor in order to confirm if I was really a Christian, and if not, I was going to die.

When we arrived at church the pastor was still at home, so they brought me to Pastor Alio's house. Shooting guns in the air, and they asked the pastor if he knew me. The pastor confirmed that I was serving among the youth and in the intercessory ministry in Paroisse Ville CECA-20. I was still without my trousers and without shoes. They said, "if this is true then everyone in the compound should contribute money" for my release. The militia took the money but refused to release me.

This time, I was taken away and they started to beat me all over. As a militia commander's vehicle came by, the militia stopped, and handed me over to the commander. They said, "Here is a Hema militia commander, take him away and deal with him as you want." I was thrown into the vehicle and sat on as though I were a bench. We drove to their center of operations.

When we arrived, I was tossed out of the vehicle. One of the militia pierced my chest with his knife on the right side. Immediately, another militia pulled out his knife and cut me on my arms. Another militia cut me on my leg while others continued to beat me. My entire body was covered with blood. I was overcome with pain and fear. In my mind I knew that my days on earth were over so I asked God to take my life.

I had been arrested around 7:00 AM, and three hours later, thrown in the dump of the militia compound as they thought I was wounded severely and about to die. Weak from the piercing, cuttings and beatings, I had no strength from the loss of blood. I stayed in the dump for about 10 hours. There were about seven dead bodies in the dump. Some bodies were already decomposing. There were also two other women still breathing, but mortally injured, waiting for their death. One of them was pregnant. Around 8:30 P.M., the militias started to entertain themselves by shooting in the air, as though they were truly fighting with their enemies.

God strengthened me physically and with a strong resolve I looked for a way to escape. I did my best to crawl out of the dump while the militia was busy firing their guns in the air. I managed to escape and walked to the seminary again where my auntie's husband was a student. I spent the rest of the night with them. The next morning I was taken to the MONUC headquarters medical center for treatment of my wounds.

Afterwards, I went to show myself in the church, because my pastor and brethren thought that I was no longer alive. When I reached "Paroisse Ville," everyone was in tears. Together we cried and praised the Lord. No one imagined that I could still be alive. After some weeks, it became impossible to live in Bunia unless one was in the militia. Fortunately the Africa Inland Mission availed their aircrafts to freely move people out of Bunia. I flew to the town of Aru, where I stayed for a year before coming back to Bunia. May all glory and honor be to God for the gift of life that He freely gives. I pray that I may always live my life for Christ, for men tried to take it, but He gave it back to me.

Salomon Mpigwa…From Boy Soldier to Man of God

I am the last born of my family. I was born on June 26, 1982 in DR Congo. I am happy that I was born in a Christian family. I am in a family of nine, with five boys and four girls in which one girl went to be with our Lord God. My father was murdered during the tribal war in the year 2000 in our country. My father was a deacon in the church, a carpenter, teacher, and also a driver.

I liked music, football and karate very much during my early age.

I am presently an undergraduate studying for a BA in Counseling Psychology at Pan African Christian University in Nairobi, Kenya. I entered the army in 1999 and left officially in 2004. This was a time of trauma and tragedy in my life that I will ever remember.

Loved Ones Lost and Loved Ones Spared

During the tribal war in 2000, in my home country and especially in my village which is called Bogoro, many people suffered. In one day more than one hundred people were killed. Among those who died I lost my friends, some members of my extended family, and my best friend who is my father, Isaac Museza. My mother was taken to be killed, but I really thank God because of His love my mother's life was spared. When she was taken they started killing others and when it was her turn to be killed, the enemies were divided into two, one group wanted to kill her and the other group wanted to interview her before they kill her.

One of their commanders knew her because one of my brothers's used to teach them music so he asked them not to kill her. Initially they would not agree with him. He said, "Do you know the woman you want to kill? Do you remember how much her son used to teach us music and we were not even paying him, let's release her, and if you don't agree with me, kill me first then you kill her." After he had said that they released my mother otherwise I would have lost both parents the same day.

We have really lost many things from that horrible day. Our house was damaged; all our property went with those merciless people. Since I have experienced such loss in my life, I have come to know that failure and pain are not easy for any one, and it does nothing to boost one's morale. Since the house was damaged, we haven't yet managed to build another house, and now my mother is living with my elder brothers. When I go home for holidays I also go to my brothers' house just because my mom does not have her own house. This is very difficult for her not to have a place to call her own home.

A Battle With Loneliness

Sometime I find myself in my room, but very far away in my mind. I spend a lot of time thinking about the death of my father and the way it has affected my life. I am not experiencing my Dad's love, and sometimes my roommate comes and asks me not to stay alone. One thing that I have come to realize is that any time I think of my lovely dad, I always spend much time alone though physically I am with others. I feel like that pain is fresh, though the years have passed.

I feel like my dad has passed away one day ago, and it always becomes more painful than before, and it makes me speechless. By the grace of my Lord God I have come to understand that, God is the father to the fatherless, and since I have come to know this truth, I really don't suffer as much as before.

How and Why I Joined the Army

Through sports and music I have made a lot of friends of different levels of thinking and professions. Among them I had friends from the army and I used to spend a lot of time with them. One of the captains became my friend. One day in the year 1999 when we were coming home from school, students were taken by soldiers by force to be trained. That was both students and young men from town who were not studying. I was one of the students who were taken.

Parents and other family members of the students were there watching their children. Some were crying and others were trying to convince the soldiers to release their children, but they would not agree with them. My mother and father were not aware that I was also taken.

My two elder brothers escaped and hid themselves from those soldiers along with others who ran to other villages or into the bush. I was able to convince my friend the captain to allow me to go home for thirty minutes to get my jacket and shoes before going to the training camp, and at first I decided with my parents urging not to go back. Other families however had lost their children to the army and I realized that I must go too. My father waived to me and I will never forget his smile. Even as I think about him now I have tears in my eyes. I didn't know I would not see him again.

In the Army a Leader of Men

In the army I was working with people older than me as well as young men my age. Once I entered the army I soon became a leader of a number of soldiers. I worked along side officers that I respected, and they in turn respected me. Life for all of us was very difficult. We sometimes lived in mountains and valleys and at that time war became the usual thing for us. Life was very hard as we often did not have food, clothes, or proper shoes. We did not have a normal place where we could live without being attacked.

We fought with the Congolese Army, the Ugandan Army, the Rwandans Army, the Interahamwe, and many other militia groups in and around Bunia. Many people lost their lives and others were wounded badly. Some of our men were paralyzed and many innocent people died.

I have come to realize that in a time of war many terrible things take place and people do things they would not do in a time of peace. Sometimes soldiers get involved in sexual immorality, the using of drugs, stealing from innocent people, and becoming liars. It is very easy to get involved in these things as you are socializing with those who do it every day.

There came a time that I was finally very tired of the conflict. I wanted the immorality to stop, and most importantly, I wanted the war to be over. I wanted to bring reconciliation and peace in my country. I thought that through music, which is a great love in my life, I could bring together different tribes and people and we could learn to communicate with melody and not bullets.

God's Grace is Great

A cease fire came in 2004 and I decided to turn over my gun to the United Nations forces. Doing so put me in danger from others who wanted to continue to fight, so I had to flee to Kenya. It was there that my life would change forever. I will always remember the day in my life that I was born again. I knew I needed God to forgive me for all the terrible things I had seen and done.

It was very difficult for me to tell someone else my problem. I met a fine Christian man who told me about God's love and His willingness to forgive me. When he asked me to repent I knew I must because my problem was really heavy for me. I was having many terrible dreams.

My mentor had great wisdom and he asked me write down everything I could remember that I had done. When we met, he told me to give him the paper. At first I had doubt, but then he told me, "I will not read your paper, but we have to burn it in the Name of Jesus," and we did so. Since that day I feel free. I have overcome my shame and guilt. I don't take it for granted but I am grateful to God for changing me. I was a soldier while still a boy, but I am determined to be a man who lives for God. I also have a new song in my heart.

The Prayer Cave...Unshakable Faith Revealed

One of the most amazing stories I heard while in Bunia in 2006 was the story of the Prayer Cave. On one campus in Bunia sits the very large sanctuary of the "La Paroisse Francophone, CECA-20 Bunia." This is the congregation of the African Inland Mission church in Bunia. I was told that some time after this very large sanctuary was built, which can seat some 1,000 people, a local Indian businessman became a Christian, and this became his home church.

As he read the Bible he came upon the teaching of the tithe. This is an Old Testament teaching that is applied even today in New Testament churches. The word simply means "tenth." In the Torah, or first five books of the Old Testament, Moses taught the people that the first ten percent of everything you earn, whether it be agricultural produce or currency, belongs to God for His work. You must learn to live on the ninety percent that is left over.

When the Indian businessman read this he realized he was quite successful and prosperous after many years as a shopkeeper, but he had never given anything to God or his work. He had spent everything on himself. He felt compelled to make amends for this and thus gave the church a substantial financial gift which was used to build a large gathering hall across the courtyard from the sanctuary. This hall is used for wedding receptions, social gatherings, and is rented out to the United Nations or other Non Government Organizations to hold meetings and a host of other functions.

In 2003 when rebel forces came through Bunia and killed, raped, and pillaged the community, many people fled. In the floor of the store room of the great gathering hall one can open a trap door, and climb down into another storage room. A number of the members of the church did just that to hide from rebel forces and declared this to be, The Prayer Cave.

The people began to pray for God to save them from this time of incredible violence and potential death. Within days the United Nations sent forces in and drove the rebels out. They set up their headquarters literally across the street from the church. Since October 2003 seven days a week, twenty four hours a day, rotating groups of people have continued to pray for the Congo in the Prayer Cave.

Women Praying in the Prayer Cave

Every December when I am back in the Congo to speak at the annual Leadership Conference I first visit the Prayer Cave to have the intercessors on duty pray for me before I speak. I find that the atmosphere in that sacred space where prayer alone occurs is literally like no other place I have ever visited. It is saturated with the presence of God.

Dr. James Seymour Coming From the Prayer Cave

Whenever I have special prayer requests for myself, my family, or my coworkers I send a message to my colleagues in the Congo to pass on my request to the Prayer Cave. I believe with all of my heart there is no greater power in the universe than the power of prayer.

Pastor Sam Alio…Three Encounters With Certain Death

I am Pastor Sam Alio. It was fifteen years ago that I began serving our Lord Jesus Christ as pastor in "Paroisse Francophone, CECA-20 Ville," in Bunia DRC. Most of the time of my ministry has been full of difficulties, or testing due to political instability and a cycle of militias, one after the other.

In 1996, the first rebellion that moved our region began but was rapidly handled. A second one arose in 1998, and by 2003, it turned into inter-tribal clashes. This was the worst of all as many people lost their lives in Bunia and its surrounding areas in the Ituri District.

Tribes that were directly involved were Hema and Lendu, that were both living in Bunia and its surrounding areas. The inter-ethnic clashes we went through spared no one. Everyone was in danger and everyone was a victim, including the church of Christ. There were assassinations, pillages, violence, harassment, trauma, hatred and many terrible things. The church lost its savor of being salt of the earth and light of the world. In fact, many church buildings were destroyed and burned.

I give thanks to the Lord because His grace and protection was evident upon my entire family. By God's grace, I am a spiritual leader, well known and influential in Bunia and Ituri district as a whole. I pastor one of the largest churches in the town of Bunia. Because of my position as a spiritual leader, some turned against me so that I was targeted for death. My life became more and more in danger beginning in the year 2003. The month of May 2003 was one of the darkest and longest periods of my life. Three times God delivered me from the hands of the militias, and several times militias fired guns over my head, or between my legs.

The whole month of May 2003, I can remember that I didn't sleep in my house more than five nights. Every night, militias visited my house so I had to spend most nights outside or in my office in the church. With time, it became impossible to hide because people flocked to my compound and in our church for safety, since we were located just some meters away from the UN headquarters.

Our facilities could not hold the number of people who flocked there so we became victims of the disease called cholera. A very bad situation was now becoming unbearable.

How could I move my family to a safer place? That was my greatest concern. Thank God, my children traveled in a convoy of Ugandan soldiers who were leaving Bunia to go back to their country. I remained back with my wife. God did a miracle for us when an AIM aircraft was sent to evacuate AIM workers, and the pilots accepted to pick my wife up as well. She joined the children in the town of Aru on the border of Uganda. I stayed alone without my family, but the weight of responsibility was still heavy on my shoulders because I could see hundreds of people in my compound and hundreds more in the church building.

The longest day of my life was on 11th May 2003. I spent the whole day and the whole night under my bed. Our quarters became the fighting field. Bombs and grenades fell on our compound, and bullets were fired into our roof, but God protected us. I can remember on that day, one of my neighbors lost two of his children as a bomb fell on their house.

In a neighboring clinic, a woman was torn up by a bomb. It was so tragic because she had just given birth. She died but the baby was miraculously saved. The next morning there was mourning everywhere in my neighborhood. All my neighbors were victims as there were dead bodies all over the place. We had no choice but to bury people collectively, using one hole for ten or more bodies. That entire week I lived on water alone as there was no food in Bunia.

It became impossible for me to remain in Bunia so my prayer was that I might leave town. Three times I was taken by militia to be killed, and each time one would change their mind and I would be able to escape to safety.

Thank God, AIM Air availed again with another aircraft to evacuate the rest of its people who remained in Bunia to the town of Aru where there was safety. My problem was how to reach the airport?

We had to walk to the airport, which is only seven kilometers away from the city center. The seven kilometers walk was like a seventy kilometers walk because of the multiple road blocks on the way, posted by various militias. We were in a convoy of more than 700 people who were all moving towards the airport.

By God's grace, I made it to Aru, but our church in Bunia never closed its doors. There were prayers everyday and every Sunday believers gathered to pray for the nation. Physically, my family was separated from the church, but we were always together in prayer. I could give them directives through cell phone calls, and they always updated me on what was going on. I was still there pastor from many kilometers away.

I stayed in Aru for 14 months, and then I returned back to Bunia on 14th July 2004, although it was not yet safe for me to be back. There was great famine in Bunia, as well as insecurity and fear. Every morning that you would wake up, you sincerely thanked God for the gift of life. We heard the call of God and we decided to come back and carry on with the ministry the Lord had entrusted us with. God has shown that He is faithful to us up until this very day.

Our great joy is that during that difficult time, God called and miraculously empowered some members of our church for ministry. He took some for theological training.

Today we rejoice and testify to the goodness of God when we see Balidja Richard, Baraka, JP Drata, James Biensi, and Nyeligudi Merry-Valentine all called to and training for the ministry.

God has done so much for us. He has shown us grace upon grace by connecting us to His faithful servants, like Dr. James Seymour and Dr. JL William, whom our local congregation, "Paroisse Ville" views as its permanent members. Though they live miles away, their hearts are in Bunia, and in our church. We also won't forget Pastor Patrick Kuchio from Kenya, whom we consider like one of our pastors. God is now using our church as an instrument to serve other churches in Bunia, and the DRC in general.

Finally, I can boldly testify that the Lord is our shepherd, even though we walk through the valley of the shadow of death, we are comforted by His active presence in our life. We are so much grateful to God for His unlimited care and favor upon us. We believe that God has got in store for us many good things, so may His name be praised forever and ever. Amen!

A HOSPITAL DESTROYED
Ahuka Ona Longombe MD, PhD.

THE CREATION OF CENTRE MEDICAL EVANGELIQUE (CME) DE NYANKUNDE

The Evangelical Medical Center (CME) of Nyankunde is a Non Government Organization created by five Christian Churches of the Eglise du Christ au Congo (ECC) since 1965. Today seven Churches of the ECC participate in the activities of CME at Nyankunde. CME received its legal status under the Presidential Order No 70-086 of March 11, 1970.

CME is localized at Nyankunde, District of the Ituri, Oriental Province, at DRC.

CME of Nyankunde served a double population; an immediate population situated around Nyankunde with an estimated 128,000 people before the war in Ituri District. The Health District of Nyankunde did have 28 stations of Health Posts and Health Centers before tribal fighting began. This population estimate now is around 13,500 people. The statistics from the administrative authorities show that at least 5,000 people died during the wars and many other people fled Nyankunde.

A distant population of the communities of Oriental, Equateur, and Kivu Provinces with approximately eight million people situated in the zones covered by about thirty health structures of the seven churches is situated mainly at the East and North of the DRC.

Outside its usual action zone, the CME also had served the French-speaking countries neighboring of the DRC, notably Rwanda, Burundi and the Central African Republic (CAR). We were a lifeline of health and hope for many.

CME Nyankunde was a specialized center with more than 250 beds providing highly specialized care for technical training of doctors and also a training center for Family Medicine. The staff encompassed specialists in Surgery, Orthopedics, Obstetrics and Gynecology, Internal Medicine and Pediatrics. It is because of the availability of these qualified professional's that difficult cases such as complications of obstructed labor, tumor surgery needing specialized care, were also referred to the CME for appropriate medical assistance. Beyond this, physicians, young doctors and nurses came from overseas for training in Tropical Medicine. The medical staff 2001 seen here.

The CME pursued five objectives in its actions:

1. To propagate the Gospel of God's Love and to help its staff, pupils, students and sick people.

2. To establish and to develop a center for medical care specializing in conditions of rural and remote environments.

3. To train and distribute the medical and paramedical staff according to its own needs and those of the communities and churches.

4. To sustain and supervise the churches-related hospitals as far as possible by medical visits, by providing medicine, and medical equipments;

5. To initiate in the communities development projects that will enhance the quality of people's lives.

The Green House Project at Nyankunde

CME Nyankunde was supervising 15 hospitals and over 50 health Centers at the East part of Democratic Republic of Congo, and Central African Republic. Many of these were remote and roads were very poor. With the help of MAF (Missionary Aviation Fellow) doctors we were able to fly to help needy people in remote areas like those seen below

Mission Aviation Fellowship Flies Doctors to Rural Areas

Patients Waiting for the Flying Doctors from Nyankunde

Senseless Violence: The Destruction of Nyankunde Hospital

It is important to note that inter-ethnic conflicts have taken a very terrible toll in Ituri District since the 1990s. In addition it is important to say that after the 1994 Rwanda genocide extremist groups fled that country to establish their residence in regions of the Eastern of DRC.

The inter-ethnic conflicts between different tribes are at the root of the unimaginable destruction at Nyankunde and the CME Hospital on September 5, 2002. The wanton destruction of both life and property was experienced on a level seldom witnessed before in the history of this nation.

On the humanitarian side more than 1,000 people were killed by bullets, knives, and other weapons. Many who were killed were our patients, workers, and those in the general population of Nyankunde. The result was massive displacement of people from Nyankunde to North Kivu   lasted several years.

Innocent People Killed at Nyankunde Massacre

On the material side there was also massive destruction of property. After 37 years of existence and development, the CME had many cars, medical facilities of great value, equipment and a big stock of medicines. The value of all this was beyond two million USA dollars. Our last inventory of the medicines alone was at least $200,000.

The cars, equipment and assorted goods of the CME were requisitioned and robbed by the militias. In addition to this, houses, hospital buildings and offices were completely destroyed.

It was a tragic and terrible day for a work that had been so lovingly built over many decades to be totally destroyed in little more than a day. A recent visit shows that the destruction reached an unimaginable level. We believe that addressing the heart issues behind the conflicts is the most urgent need.

Hospital buildings before militias' destruction

Hospital buildings after militias' destruction

The buildings that gave life and hope were destroyed by hatred and violence. The term "mindless destruction" seems to apply to the destruction of the hospital at Nyankunde. Here was a place where babies were born and the sick found healing. To destroy this place of hope seems to be madness. The burning of the Nursing School where health care workers were trained, and the thriving agricultural projects that provided food for the campus and community, appears to be acts of absolute self-destruction. The prayer of many is the rebuilding of the Medical Center at Nyankunde.

Nursing College Graduations Service

Before the Destruction

The Nurses training school at Nyankunde was one of the crown jewels of the work there. Many young women were trained by skilled doctors and instructors to minister to the unique and varied medical needs of the patients who came to their door. In the aftermath of this terrible destruction of the Nursing College smaller programs have been set up in other communities including Bunia to try and continue to meet the needs of the people of Ituri District.

Destruction of the Nursing College

The ghastly wounds to the medical buildings and Nursing College have broken the hearts of the people of Ituri District. The question is asked but not answered effectively; "How could anyone destroy the hospital where they themselves were likely born and their loved one's cared for in times of sickness?" The heart of man is clearly capable of

PART III

HUMANITARIAN INTERVENTIONS

Chapter 5

THE DORCAS CLUB

War and suffering are not selective. They destroy homes and property and disrupt the balance of life for everybody within their orbit. In the aftermath of the war in the Congo the February 29, 2008 UN Commission on the Status of Women states that as many as 40% of the women of the DRC are widows and that 43% of the heads of households are now women. Some entire villages are comprised of women and children as the men have been killed in warfare. Addressing this reality has become our priority.

One of the first projects launched by Accumulated Resources of Kindred Spirits (ARKS), the non profit organization that I serve as

Executive Director, was the formation of the Dorcas Club. While in the Congo in 2006 and seeing the needs of widows I found that for $60.00 I could purchase a Chinese made sewing machine. I purchased the first one for a pastor's wife with some funds provided by my mother-in-law, Mrs. Iona DeGroat. She is a fine sewer and I thought she would be pleased to provide a machine for a pastor's wife to help provide for her family.

I then realized if we had ten machines we could create a program to teach women to sew, and upon completion of the program provide them with their own machine to help support their families. I shared this concept when I returned from Africa and the first two men I told about my plan, Phil Bradley and George Mills, together gave me $600.00 to buy the ten machines and we were in business. I sent the funds to Pastor Jean Marc in the Congo via Western Union, and we set up the program in the local church.

The Dorcas Club Sewing Program for Widows

I was present for the second graduation of the Dorcas Club in December of 2007. Typically they train eighteen widows from nine different churches for three months. At graduation they receive both a diploma and their own machine. During the three months of training they must earn $20.00 to contribute to their machine and I raise the other $40.00 so we have a two to one match and the sense of investment in oneself.

It was a graduation like none other. Over a thousand people attended and cheered as the women danced down the aisle of the church in lovely matching dresses that they had made in class. The atmosphere was charged with joy.

Upon receiving their certificate and new sewing machine after the graduation service graduates walked home with the sewing machine perfectly balanced on their heads. What a proud moment of achievement and hope.

Dorcas Club Graduation 2007

Graduates march into the auditorium in matching dresses that they had sown and singing as they come. As they walk on stage to get their certificates the audience cheers.

Graduates receive a certificate and their own sewing machine to support themselves and their children

By teaching these lovely women to sew and helping them to obtain their own sewing machine we are empowering them to change the reality of both themselves and their children. The also have the experience of rebuilding their sense of self worth. Women have suffered the theft of their security and their sense of significance at the hands of brutal men. The chance to write a new chapter in their life story which includes self sufficiency is a great joy indeed.

Chapter 6

HOPE FELLOWSHIP

Orphan care continues to be a great challenge all across the continent of Africa and in many other places around the world. HIV/AIDS has left sub Saharan Africa with 17 million deaths and 12 million orphans. In Bunia the orphan crisis has been exacerbated by the terrible number of war casualties.

One of the small attempts to address the orphan issue in Bunia was to extend a challenge to church members to take an orphan into their home with the promise that I would then raise the funds for school fees. Primary school education is not free in most African nations. Education is highly prized but not all can afford to pay for their studies. A year of primary school education is around $100.00 in USA currency.

Initially ten families accepted my challenge and took into their homes ten orphans and we raised the $1,000 for their fees. After two years there are now fifty families who have responded and the challenge is now for me to raise $5,000 per year. Somehow I have found that people of good will are quick to respond to the needs of those less fortunate and with each new challenge of a new child in need of school fees, another person steps forward to meet that need. I find this very encouraging.

Children of the Hope Fellowship

Many of these beautiful smiling faces have been stained with tears as mothers and fathers have died as the result of war and its aftermath. Being taken into a loving family and now having the chance to go to school and get an education seems to be a dream come true for these precious little ones. For $100 you could change a life for a year through the gift of formal education.

Pastor Jean Marc and the Hope Fellowship Children

Pastor Jean Marc is a loving and caring Shepherd who display's kindness and compassion to these orphans. Having experienced the bitter fruits of war in his own family this gentle man is totally invested in the wellbeing of these children of Africa.

Chapter 7

THE HOUSE OF GRACE

Dr. Seymour with the children of the House of Grace

Street children are an ever present presence in the town of Bunia. Everywhere one walks there are children who walk along side you asking for money as they say they are hungry. I am sure that they are. One attempt to address this ever present need is through the work of the House of Grace.

Our ARKS worker in the Congo, Jean Paul Drata, who is a graduate of Pan African Christian University in Nairobi, Kenya where I first met him, wrote the following report on this work of compassion. Here is Jean Paul's perspective.

After the devastating war in DRC, several attempts have been made to care for street children in Bunia. Unfortunately, many of them have failed. It is evident that the House of Grace is succeeding. It continues to attract street boys as it provides them with a secure environment and has facilitated the return of several boys to their families. The House of Grace began in 2005 with ten street children. The number has currently increased to over 50.

While living on the street, the children were involved in theft, drugs, drinking and sniffing gasoline. A few children were also child soldiers in the recent war years. This life style resulted in emotional problems for many.

A New Arrival at the House of Grace

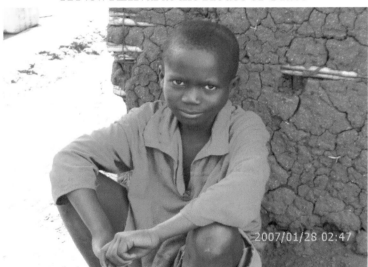

The House of Grace actually consists of a collection of buildings on a small sloping piece of land near to the road. The property is unfenced and completely open to passers-by. It backs onto the river where people bring their vehicles to wash. Behind and by the side of the plot are a few private houses and a small grinding house. There is some attempt to grow a few vegetables on the edge of the plot near the well. The buildings consist of sleeping quarters built of adobe brick and tin roof, a small cook-house, latrines, and a covered well.

A larger dormitory building made of more durable materials has been recently completed. This has been made possible by a generous financial gift from the Farrell Foundation in the USA. New bunk beds and a grinding machine for corn and cassava were made possible by another generous gift from the people of Grace Bible Fellowship in Cary, North Carolina in the USA. The boys received last Christmas a set of new clothes and new soccer balls from Heaven Sent Adoptions also of Raleigh, North Carolina, in order to play soccer on a near-by piece of ground.

Since the children had all dropped out of school, Pastor Djadri the leader of the center, has made it a priority to send them back to school. He is also trying to reintegrate them with their families or relatives. This is very crucial because the House of Grace is not a permanent Orphanage, but rather a transitional home. It is very impressive the way Pastor Djadri interacts with the children.

He cares for them with deep faith, love, devotion and patience. Due to this the children call him "Mwalimu," a Swahili word which means teacher.

Pastor Djadri and Jean Paul Drata

Every day Pastor Djadri has a Bible study and devotion time with the children, teaching them the Word of God in order to help the children grow spiritually, and become good members of their community.

As a result of spending time with the children and teaching them the Word of God, these children are learning to share their confidential problems. Twenty two children gave their lives to Christ and are candidates for baptism. Recently we have created the House of Grace choir in order to make the center a blessing to local churches.

Also helping at the center is Mama Lucy who is a widow. She is the one cooking the food for the children. Besides preparing the food every day, she also educates the children in social matters and teaches them health and hygiene. She is the "mother figure" of the House of Grace. She intervenes when the children fight just like any mom.

Mama Lucy

Another member of the team is Jean, who himself was living on the streets. Pastor Djadri invited him to come and work at the center while at the same time completing his adults' secondary education. Jean stays with the boys at night and is like their elder brother, playing football with them and spending time with them.

Jean…the big brother for all the boys

Why Children Join the Streets

There are two major reasons for the children living on the streets. The first is related to family problems and the second is in connection with the war.

Family Reasons

Most children left their families to join the street life because they were physically and psychologically abused at home. Many had been badly beaten, denied food and restricted to their homes. Others joined the street because during the tribal conflict, children of mixed Lendu and Hema marriages were rejected by both parents, and forced by their parents to live on the streets.

Some children had no one to care for them when their parents died of natural causes. Others lived with relatives after the death of their parents, but joined the streets when life with their relatives became too difficult. There were also some who were rejected by step-parents when the mother or father remarried.

War Reasons

Some children were separated from their parents at the outbreak of the war. Children and parents were forced to take different routes when they fled from the fighting, leaving children with no choice but to join the street life and struggle to survive. It is a tragic situation for all.

Special Cases in Need of Grace

Two of the children in the center had been soldiers. One of them is now 14 years old and the other one is now 10. The one who is 14 has a special problem of bedwetting so he has many problems with the other boys who do not appreciate this behavior. In order to help him in a practical way we bought him a watch with an alarm clock. This watch wakes him up every night at the same time so he can go to the toilet. He told Pastor Djadri that ever since he had the watch he has not wet the bed.

Another street child was rejected by his biological father and his stepmother because they suspected him of involvement with black magic. His father told Pastor Djadri that his wife, the street child's step mother, had a vision which identified his black magic. The father wanted to take his son to a pastor who would cast out the demons from the child. Pastor Djadri declined to send him to this pastor because during the two years that the boy has been at the center he has not shown any sign of being possessed. He is a devoted Christian and he truly believes in God. The child himself said he was never involved in black magic. Such are the conflicts of a child in crisis in Africa.

Former Boy Soldiers at the House of Grace

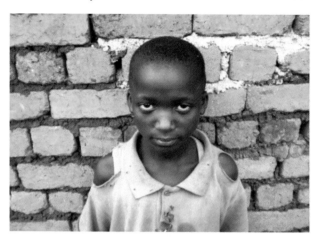

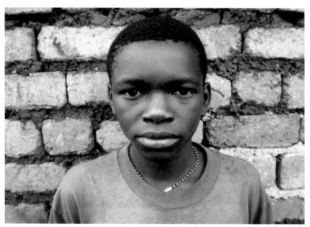

To live with and take care of children who are traumatized in so many ways is difficult. We have been trying to meet all the conditions of living with them. We have shared our spiritual and social lives with the boys, and that brings about incredible change. The change we witness in their lives is God working in them, and also a result of showing them love, compassion, concern, and spiritual commitment on our part.

The center has 51 street children, and the number is increasing. Up to 50 more street children come to the facility periodically. The need continues to grow for a loving and safe place for those who have no home to call their own. Since August 2007, eleven children have rejoined their families or relatives, thus leaving space for newcomers.

Another challenge is that of finances. Some of the children's' family members live far away from where the center is located. If a child wants to join his family or his family wants to collect him from the center, the plan fails for lack of money for transportation.

There are children who do not have any relatives to live with, therefore it would be helpful to find host-families to accept and take care of a street child. Such foster parents would need instruction in caring for these boys. All in all the task of re-socializing street children is huge. It is not possible for one person to do it alone. It demands cooperation between local and international organizations.

When these children were living on the street they were very aggressive because they had to survive. Now they are living in a new environment where aggression is not allowed. However, fighting happens among them sometimes because change of behavior is a long process and needs to be directed with consistency. There is also a need to develop recreation for them in order to help them discharge their energy in playing games and lessen the conflict and fighting.

Beans and Rice for Lunch at the House of Grace

Chapter 8

NEW PARADIGMS IN FUNDING: BRICKS AND BISCUITS

The Kingdom Brick Company

One of the challenges of funding humanitarian projects in the developing world is what is called "donor fatigue." At some point in time even generous donors begin to ask the question, "Will my giving ever be enough to meet the overwhelming needs of the people?" My commitment is not to create long term dependency, but rather to empower people to the greatest extent possible, to take care of themselves. One project I am working on in the Congo is the development of the Kingdom Brick Company.

With a generous grant from the Farrell Foundation we were able to purchase from South Africa a Hydraform Brick Making Machine. This product was invented in 1988 by Jochen Kofahl and Robert Plattner in a garage in South Africa. Today the company has offices in South Africa, Uganda, Nigeria, and India. Upgrades and design development has been done in conjunction with Witts University in South Africa. The machine is being used in over fifty countries with remarkable success.

The machine operates with a diesel motor and produces over 1,000 interlocking blocks per day. The blocks are made of five percent cement, mixed with gravel and soil and compressed in the machine. This is an environmentally friendly way to build as no trees are destroyed to burn a kiln.

Hydraform Brick Machine

New Bricks Being Watered to Cure in Bunia

Jean Paul Drata building a house with Kingdom Bricks

The Gathering Place

Another project that ARKS has invested in is a kiosk at a petrol station. Our Director of Operation Bunia is a very fine young man, Jean Paul Drata. He graduated in 2007 from Pan African Christian University and returned to Bunia to oversee our humanitarian projects. We provided Jean Paul with a motorcycle, a lap top computer, a printer and a small monthly salary.

We also invested funds to help Jean Paul to begin his own small business which could help in his personal support, and ARKS would remain a ten percent partner. Each month ten percent of the profits for the kiosk are put into the Compassion Fund of the Operation Bunia account. These funds are used for needs that arrive such as the purchase of a bride price cow for a young man who wanted to marry or financial assistant for a pastor whose mother had died. The Gathering Place is a venue where people can buy biscuits, bread, soda and soap. It is also a place that helps to support projects to help struggling people to survive.

Jean Paul and His Employees at The Gathering Place

Chapter 9

MICRO-FINANCING TO EMPOWER THE POWERLESS

Poverty in Africa effects both urban and rural dwellers. Some 70% of the continents 900 million people live in rural areas where the vast majority is poor. Most financial services in Africa are found in urban settings. It is estimated that only 5% of the 630 million African people living in rural settings have access to any form of financial services.

One of the greatest economic developments of the last two decades is the discovery of the effectiveness of micro financing to the poor. The pioneer in this field is 2006 Nobel Peace Prize winner Muhammad Yunus, the founder of Grameen Bank in Bangledesh. Yunus pioneered microcredit, the innovative banking program that provides poor people—mainly women—with small loans they use to launch businesses and lift their families out of poverty. In the past thirty years microcredit has spread to every continent and benefited over 100 million families.

Dr. Yunus began very small in his attempt to help the poor to become self sufficient. In 1976 he was a young economics professor and the Head of the Rural Economics Program at the University of Chittagong in Bangladesh. He became very frustrated that none of the wonderful theories of economics that he and his colleagues were teaching and discussing had true application among the poor of the nation.

He went out and made a list of all the very poor people he knew. He had 42 people on his list and after talking to them he determined that all of them put together needed a total of $27 to improve their situation. So he loaned them each the money they needed out of his own pocket. They each paid the money back and improved their life.

One person he assisted was a lady who made bamboo chairs. She did not have the few cents needed to buy the materials to make her chairs each day. So she borrowed the money from a money lender who required that she sell her chairs to him at a drastic discount to the market. This kept her in a poverty trap of never being able earn enough money to buy her own materials and sell her chairs at market price and thus earn a much more livable wage.

Dr. Yunus loaned her the money to buy the materials herself and from the profits she made by selling her chairs at the market price she was able to pay back her loan and break out of the poverty trap. This was the beginning of GRAMEEN BANK which was founded by Dr. Yunus as a project in 1976, and formally become a bank in 1983. By 2008 the bank has had a total of 6.61 million borrowers 97 per cent of which are women. The bank has 2,226 branches. It works in 71,371 villages with a total staff of 18,795.

The amount of loans disbursed by Grameen Bank, since inception, is US$ 5.72 billion and $5.07 billion has been repaid. Currently they have outstanding loans of $ 457.52 million.

Women Seem to be the Key in Micro Finance Projects

Another leader in microfinance is Opportunity International, a non-profit organization dedicated to helping the poor. They provide financial services to the poor and train them in basic business practices so that they can work their way out of poverty. They have developed the Trust Group model which has brought success to millions of poor entrepreneurs around the world. Under this model loans are given to groups of people who monitor each other in the repayment of the loan. Each one is responsible to pay their part regularly or their colleagues must pay it for them. This group accountability has proven to be very effective indeed.

Operation Bunia is launching into this area of service to the poor of the community with a two tier approach which provides training first to develop a business plan. Then loans to both individuals and small groups are possible beginning with $50.00 to $100.00. This loan must be repaid at 10% interest on a specific timeline and then a second larger loan can be applied for.

The goal always is to empower people to take care of themselves and their loved ones. Research on micro financing around the world reveals that the poor will indeed repay their loans on time and with diligence. The issue is not interest on a loan, but access to a loan that is the heart of the matter.

It is also potentially the hope of young adults.

Children are the immediate beneficiaries of working parents.

Chapter 10

A CONVERSATION AT 30,000 FEET

While flying to Zimbabwe, Africa in May of 2008 I got up around 3:00 AM as I was no longer able to endure the seats, and was simply unable to sleep. As I endeavored to stretch my sore muscles I went to stand for a while back in the galley where I met a very interesting African gentleman.

After exchanging complaints about how hard it is to sleep on an airplane the older one gets we began to share our thoughts as only strangers might in the middle of the night at 30,000 feet. He asked me why I was headed to Africa and I shared my love for the continent and her people. I told him of my twelve years of living in Africa and how my three children grew up in Zimbabwe. I told him of my youngest daughter who was born in Africa and now lived in Madagascar where she and her husband ran an orphanage and a mobile clinic. I also shared about my work in the Democratic Republic of Congo.

He told me he was returning from a University graduation of his daughter in Washington, DC, and was now heading to meetings in Mozambique for financial leaders of African nations. It was then that Mr. J.C. Masangu Mulongo shared with me that he was the Governor of the Central Bank of the Democratic Republic of Congo. With sincerity and passion he told of his love for his country and his pride in his people as they were courageously rebuilding their nation after the terrible recent years of war.

With clarity and insight he outlined the necessary steps toward building a strong nation on the ashes of suffering. The challenges for development and stability in the Congo are of course daunting. Here was a man helping to lead the way.

The International Committee of the Red Cross (ICRC) made the following observations in there June 12, 2007 report. Although it was a general statement based on the research and observation of eighty field workers around the world, it could have been a report specifically applied to the Democratic Republic of Congo. Excerpts from the report are as follows.

Analysis of the dynamics of armed conflicts around the world is as delicate an undertaking as ever. Experience shows that the roots of most present-day armed conflicts lie in a combination of factors at the local or national level. In the past, they would have mostly pitted two or more rulers, be it of chiefdoms or countries, against one another with the aim of gaining influence or territorial control.

Such conflicts involved conventional, established and structured armed forces, which clashed on designated battlefields, with front lines that could be marked on equally conventional maps. These armed confrontations sought to obtain by force what the warring parties could not achieve by dialogue or negotiation.

As we head further into the 21st century patterns of warfare are evolving. Fewer wars are being fought for outright control of territory, although there are, of course, some that have a strong territorial dimension or undercurrent, such as the Israeli–Palestinian conflict. Fewer wars are being fought for deep-seated ideological reasons, as they were during the Cold War.

Nowadays, conflicts appear to be more often fueled by pressure to secure immediate and long-term access to or control over key natural resources. Economic factors therefore play a significant role with armed elements indulging in economic implications. Many countries meanwhile continue to suffer from inherently weak or collapsed public services, such as health, water and social welfare.

Such developments have been complicated by a number of other factors: the assertion of identity; weapon proliferation, environmental degradation and scarcity of land and water; mass migration leading to an increase in new forms of urban violence; and in several contexts, the blurring of the line between political violence and criminal activity.

Another feature of current conflict environments is the variety of forms of confrontation involving the interplay of local, regional and global dynamics. By 2007 there remained few wars between States but a growing number of highly complex non-international armed conflicts involving a diversity of actors with a variety of grievances and acquiring at times, an international dimension.

There has been a marked rise in influence of non-State actors, specifically those engaging in armed violence. Such groups are often unstable and have a tendency to fragment into different sub factions, which regroup under new commands. In 2007 several armed groups were engaged in a confrontation on a global scale with a number of States. This manifested itself in several countries mainly in acts of "terrorism," on the one hand, and counter-terrorism operations, on the other hand.

Situations of armed conflict are frequently characterized by their extended duration, chronic nature, generally low intensity and widespread impact. Whether an armed conflict or situation of violence, the outcome is inevitably that large numbers of people are killed, injured, detained, separated from their families or missing. Moreover, many people are also affected indirectly, such as the sick being unable to access medical care because of the fighting or insecurity.

A 2007 Red Cross report suggested that there are two key challenges in responding to today's armed conflicts and other situations of violence: one is to have a clear understanding of the diversity of armed conflicts and other situations of violence and the specificity of each; and the other is to address in a meaningful way the multitude of needs faced by the affected populations.

Bringing Home the Children of War

One of the challenges in the healing of the Congo is the integration of both boys and girls who became combatants during the years of tribal warfare. Many were forcibly taken from their schools and their homes and trained in the bush to fight with a militia, usually established along tribal lines.

These young men and women saw human suffering and violence at its most fundamental level and many were participants in inflicting terrible suffering on innocent people themselves. An estimated 30,000 boys and girls were abducted and put into the militia. They were not old enough to vote but were old enough to carry a gun.

The social network's of family interaction was broken down over the years of absence from home. These children have fallen behind in their education, have lost the skills of living within a family unit, and have often learned to respond to life's disappointment with violence. The people of the community to which they return may also look at these children with both fear and contempt. A process of reintegration will take time as trust and good will must be reestablished by many.

Young Girl Soldier in Congo War

The United Nations Report on Children Soldiers Reported

- The use of rape and sexual violence as a tactic of war – and the impunity afforded to its perpetrators – pose a particular risk to young girls in conflict zones. In the DRC, for example, children account for a startling 33 per cent of all rape victims.

- Representatives of 58 countries met in Paris in February 2007 and committed themselves to putting an end to the unlawful recruitment and use of children in armed conflicts. The Paris conference, hosted by the Government of France and UNICEF, brought together both countries affected by the use of child soldiers as well as donor nations to tackle the recruitment of children and to harness the political will to confront it.

- The "Paris Principles and Guidelines on children associated with armed groups" establish two ways to address the issue of child soldiers: (1) build a serious international commitment to abolish the practice; and (2) make sure that commitment is translated into real, ongoing protection for children and their families as they resume civilian life. In October 2007, seven more countries joined the original 58 who had approved the guidelines to subscribe to good practices in ending the use of children in armed conflict.

Reestablishment of Agriculture in an Environment of Safety

Agriculture is central to the lives of the 67 percent of Congolese living in rural areas. Due to the conflicts of recent years, there are still 1.6 million people who are displaced and up to 40,000 per month still fleeing their homes due to dangers. Many had to run away leaving burning houses and all of their possessions. Herds of cattle and other livestock as well as crops ready to be harvested have all been abandoned as people have had to escape to save their very lives.

A primary challenge in DRC today is to get people back to their homes in order to rebuild their lives. This is a very difficult task as some fear to return to the place of terror and others have returned only to find that strangers now inhabit their land. Even though there have been treaties of peace signed the situation remains unstable.

For example on June 7, 2008 there was a deadly attack by rebels on a makeshift camp in the Rutshuru area of North Kivu province. The raid on Kinyandoni camp left at least nine people dead and scores wounded. The camp shelters some 5,000 internally displaced people. UN officials blame the murderous attack on the rebel Democratic Forces for the Liberation of Rwanda.

Apparently several armed men stormed the camp stealing mobile telephones and cash. As they left witnesses say the rebels started shooting indiscriminately at people in the camp, including a group of children who were playing. In light of such deadly situations that can erupt at any moment of the day or night in the Eastern part of the DRC, it is incredibly difficult to create a sense of peace and security for the people.

Is There Hope for Lasting Peace?

The skeptics might throw up their hands and say that the Democratic Republic of Congo and all of Africa are in a hopeless state. Post colonial instability and treachery by unprincipled leaders who are more committed to tribalism, nepotism, personal wealth and power than to nationalism, seems to be the norm.

My observation leads me to conclude that the hope of the future is clearly not to be found in the practices of the past. The hope of the future rests with at least four primary factors; (1) the continued development of the democratic process of free and fair elections followed by moral leadership; (2) the development of the vast natural resources of DRC for the good of the nation and not a few individuals; (3) the education of the children; (4) improvement of public health issues.

The Presidential Elections of 2006

As stated in chapter two, general elections were held in the Democratic Republic of the Congo on July 30, 2006. These were the first multiparty elections in the country in 46 years. Voters went to the polls to elect both a new President of the Republic and a new National Assembly, the lower-house of the Parliament.

Over 25 million people registered to vote for the elections in a country where the exact population is not known, but is likely in excess of 60 million. The Independent Electoral Commission (CEI or La Commission Electorale Indépendante) reported a voter turnout of 80 percent. Thirty three people registered as candidates for the Presidency and 9,000 for the 500 seats in the Federal Parliament. The initial presidential favorites were Joseph Kabila, the incumbent, and Jean-Pierre Bemba, one of the four vice-presidents.

On August 20, the CEI released its full provisional presidential election results, indicating that neither candidate was able to secure a majority, which led to a run-off election on October 29. On November 15, the CEI released its full provisional results for the presidential elections second round, indicating that Kabila had won. The results were, however, rejected by Bemba who claimed irregularities. On November 27, the DRC Supreme Court confirmed that Kabila had won the election.

Bemba left Congo for Portugal in April of 2007 after clashes between his supporters and government forces killed more than 200 people. Bemba was arrested in Belgium on May 24, 2008 for war crimes he allegedly committed in the Central African Republic. The International Criminal Court says his forces carried out a series of rapes and murders in that nation between October 2002 and March 2003.

The point is that even though the most recent elections in DRC may have been imperfect, according to international observers they were overall both free and fair. With an 80% turnout of eligible voters this is a very positive sign that the seeds of democracy are beginning to germinate and take root in people's hearts in this lush African nation.

Natural Resources and the Environment

As previously noted the DRC is the third largest country in Africa and is endowed with vast potential wealth. It is rich in minerals, has fertile land and enormous areas of rainforest. More than 74% of the country is forested, although the forests are shrinking fast, its rivers offer abundant hydroelectric potential.

Mineral Resources

The rich mineral resources of DRC include cobalt, copper, cadmium, petroleum, industrial and gem diamonds, gold, silver, zinc, manganese, tin, germanium, uranium, radium, bauxite, iron ore, coal. With proper management and development of these riches in the soil this nation could well become the single richest on the continent of Africa. The goal however must be that all of the people will benefit from these resources and not just a wealthy few.

Education for Millions of Children

DRC has 58 million people with 47.2 % under the age of 15. Only 56 percent of women in the DRC know how to read. One organization from the United States that is bringing hope is USAID which seeks to improve access to and quality of basic education, especially for girls.

USAID is also training teachers via radio and internet based programs. Radio programs also broadcast messages on the importance of girls' education to local communities. Scholarships to vulnerable girls complement these activities. Over 11,000 primary school girls received scholarships for the 2003-2004 school year and the program expands each year.

Improvement of Public HealthCare

Life expectancy for men and women is only 46 and 51 years, respectively. Many of the estimated 45,000 people per month who die in the Democratic Republic of Congo each month die of largely preventable diseases. Illnesses such as malaria, diarrhea, pneumonia, and malnutrition are prematurely ending the lives of scores of people especially children. Children comprise 19% of the population of DRC but 47% of the deaths.

Malaria is the single biggest child killer in Africa. Young children between six months and five years are especially in danger of dying from malaria because their bodies haven't yet developed immunity against the disease. Pregnant women are also more likely to become infected. It took almost 40 years before the rich countries realized that malaria is not only a dangerous disease but also a huge obstacle to successful development.

Despite all the efforts to overcome malaria, the disease remains the leading cause of death in the Democratic Republic of the Congo. According to World Bank findings it is estimated that 97 percent of DRC's 58.3 million people are at risk of endemic malaria.

The remaining three percent are vulnerable to epidemic malaria. Malaria is the number one killer of children in DRC, accounting for approximately 40% of child deaths. Distribution of treated mosquito nets is one simple but effective way to cut down on the incidents of malaria in Africa. UNICEF estimates that only around 1 in 10 children under five years old sleep under a mosquito net in DRC.

Access to Clean Water

It is estimated that one out of every five Congolese children will have had diarrhea in any given week, because only 29% of the rural population has access to clean water and less than 30% of the population have access to adequate sanitation. Over 1 in 10 child deaths are due to diarrhea. In addition, there are cholera epidemics every year in some provinces, with more than 20,000 cases per year.

The British Department for International Development is one organization that is seeking to help the DRC in this crucial need for clean water. DFID support so far has enabled 72,000 people to access clean water. Their contribution to the DRC humanitarian pooled fund has also assisted in providing water and sanitation to over 500,000 people and helped approximately 350,000 others gain permanent access to drinking water.

The most urgent water and sanitation needs are those in rural areas. Working with the UN Children's Agency (UNICEF) DFID is supporting the government of DRC's rural water and sanitation program called Village Assaini or "Clean Village".

The goal is to provide access to clean water and sanitation for 3.3 million Congolese. The program will focus on providing appropriate technical solutions. In most cases communities will be assisted to protect springs which are simple and cheap, and on providing toilets and hygiene education.

HIV/AIDS in the DRC

The Democratic Republic of the Congo has more than one million people estimated to be living with HIV/AIDS. Although the DRC's HIV/AIDS prevalence rate is still relatively low compared to the sub-Saharan African region overall, this low-income country is in a post-conflict period and faces numerous challenges including HIV/AIDS.

The spread of this deadly virus in Congo is largely through heterosexual intercourse. With the staggering amount of rape and violence against women in this nation one of the steps towards stopping the spread of AIDS and other Sexually Transmitted Diseases is to apply the harshest forms of legal punishment on those who sexually assault women and children.

Leaders With Integrity are Essential to Africa's Future

A Final Word of Hope

It is my firm conviction that perseverance is the key to successful living. In that the people of Africa seem to have perfected the art of perseverance through years of struggle I choose to believe that the future will be far better than the past. Through a partnership based on our common humanity we in the Western world have both a moral obligation and wonderful opportunity to assist our African friends in their journey to wholeness. Let us not allow ourselves to rationalize that these are not our problems. Rather let's join hands and begin our walk forward towards peace on earth and good will towards all.

END NOTES

1   American Journal of International Law, Vol. 15, No. 4, Supplement: Official Documents (Oct., 1921), 314-321.

2   Berlin Conference of 1884-1885 to Divide Africa Colonization of the Continent by European Powers   By Matt Rosenberg,

3   *The Scramble for Africa,* Chamberlain, M.E., Hong Kong: Longman Group Ltd., 1974.

4   *The Horizon: History of Africa,* American Heritage Publishing Co., New York, 1971

5   The European Scramble History of Congo:

    by Ch. Didier Gondola (Author) 2002

6   The Troubled Heart of Africa: A History of the Congo

    by Robert B. Edgerton Publisher: St. Martin's Press; 1st edition, 2002

7   The Democratic Republic of Congo: From Peace Rhetoric to Sustainable Political Stability? by Jideofor Adibe (Editor)

    Adonis & Abbey Publishers Ltd (July 21, 2007)

8   Nicky Oppenheimer, De Beers Chairman, addressing the Commonwealth Business Forum, Johannesburg, South Africa, 11 November 1999.

9   In Congo, Dark Heart of Mineral Exploitation

    by Adam Hochschild December 26, 2004

10 Hochschild, Adam Published on Sunday, December 26, 2004 by the International Herald Tribune

11 The Illegal Exploitation of Natural Resources in the Democratic Republic of Congo: A Case Study on Corporate Complicity in Human Rights Abuses Global Law Working Paper 01/05

Symposium - 'Transnational Corporations and Human Rights' by Asimina-Manto Papaioannou

NYU School of Law • New York, NY 10012

12 Banker To The Poor: Micro-Lending and the Battle Against World Poverty   1999, 2003, 2007 Perseus Book Group, NY

by Muhammad Yunus (Author)

13 Yanus, Muhammad 2003 Banker to the Poor

14 Opportunity International's Micro Insurance Agency to Develop and Provide Life, Health and Crop Insurance for 21 Million Poor People Press Release: Oak Brook, Ill. – Feb. 6, 2008

15 US AID Report 2007 on Sub Saharan Africa: The Democratic Republic of Congo

16 Child Soldiers, Global Report 2008

17 USAID Report on Sub Sahara Africa: The Democratic Republic of Congo, 2008

WORKS CITED

Adibe, Iideofor
The Democratic Republic of Congo: From Peace Rhetoric to Sustainable Political Stability?
Adonis & Abbey Publishers Ltd (July 21, 2007)

Amnesty International Report 2008
Democratic Republic of Congo: Children at War
Date Published: 9 September 2003
Categories: Africa, Central Africa, Democratic Republic Of Congo, United Nations

Allen, Karen
Bleak Future for Congo's Child Soldiers
BBC News, Masisu, Democratic Republic of Congo
25 July 2006
Coalition to Stop the Use of Child Soldiers
Global Report, 2008

de Blij, H.J. and Peter O. Muller Geography: Realms, Regions, and Concepts. John Wiley & Published on Sunday, December 26, 2004 by the International Herald Tribune

Edgerton, Robert B.
The Troubled Heart of Africa: A History of the Congo
Publisher: St. Martin's Press; 1st edition, 2002
Gondola, Didier
The European Scramble
History of Congo: 2002 Wikipedia

Hochschild, Adam
In Congo, Dark Heart of Mineral Exploitation
Published on Sunday Dec. 26, 2004 by the International Herald
Tribune

Hochschild, Adam "King Leopold's Ghost: A Story of Greed, Terror
and Heroism in Colonial Africa."
1998, First Mariners Books Edition

Human Rights News
DR Congo: Army Should Stop Use of Child Soldiers
Brussels, April 19, 2007

Nest, Michael Wallace, Grignon, Francois, Kisangani, Emizet F. The
Democratic Republic of Congo: Economic Dimensions of War and
Peace (International Peace Academy Occasional Paper)

Nzongola-Ntalaja, George
The Congo: From Leopold to Kabila: A People's History 2002,
London: Zed Press

Oppenheimer, Nicky De Beers Chairman, addressing the Commonwealth Business Forum, Johannesburg, South Africa, 11 November
1999.

Opportunity International's Micro Insurance Agency to Develop and
Provide Life, Health and Crop Insurance for 21 Million Poor People
Press Release: Oak Brook, Ill. – Feb. 6, 2008

Operational Update:
Democratic Republic of the Congo: Update on ICRC activities in the Kivus – January and February 2008
Papaioannou, Asimina-MantoThe Illegal Exploitation of Natural Resources in the Democratic Republic of Congo: A Case Study on Corporate Complicity in Human Rights Abuses Global Law Working Paper 01/05
Symposium - 'Transnational Corporations and Human Rights' NYU School of Law • New York, NY 10012
Rosenberg, Matt
Berlin Conference of 1884-1885 to Divide Africa Colonization of the Continent by European Powers
The History of Microfinance
Global Envision
Posted on April 14, 2006

US Department of State
Country Reports on Human Rights Practices - 2006
Released by the Bureau of Democracy, Human Rights, and Labor March 6, 2007

US AID Report on Sub Sahara Africa: The Democratic Republic of Congo, 2008

Yunus, Muhammad
Banker To The Poor: Micro-Lending and the Battle Against World Poverty 1999, 2003, 2007 Perseus Book Group, NY

AUTHOR OVERVIEW

Victoria Falls Zimbabwe, Africa

Dr. James Seymour is the Chair of the Department of Philosophy and Religion at Saint Augustine's College in Raleigh, North Carolina. He is also the Executive Director of an international non profit organization, Accumulated Resources of Kindred Spirits (ARKS). He has been an Ordained Minister with the General Council of the Assemblies of God since 1976.

James Seymour and his wife Dawn spent sixteen years living outside the continental United States, first in Bethel, Alaska, and then for twelve years in Zimbabwe, Africa. They have served in ministerial, educational, and humanitarian endeavors for over 30 years. The Seymour's have three married children, Jessica Johnson, Aaron Seymour, and Heather Saintmyire, plus five grandchildren; Isaac, Gabriel, Sophia, Isabelle, and Josiah. The entire Seymour family is committed to interracial and cross cultural healing, and sharing the love of God by serving others.

Printed in the United States
135091LV00001B